50 Blender Recipes for Home

By: Kelly Johnson

Table of Contents

Morning Energizers:

- Sunrise Citrus Smoothie
- Green Goddess Detox Blend
- Berry Burst Breakfast Bowl

Smoothie Bowls Galore:

- Tropical Paradise Bowl
- Acai Berry Bliss Bowl
- Peanut Butter Power Bowl

Refreshing Cold Soups:

- Chilled Cucumber Gazpacho
- Spicy Watermelon Mint Soup
- Creamy Avocado Lime Soup

Savory Dips and Spreads:

- Roasted Red Pepper Hummus
- Spinach and Artichoke Dip
- Zesty Black Bean Salsa

Creative Nut Butters:

- Vanilla Almond Bliss Butter
- Chocolate Hazelnut Heaven
- Maple Pecan Delight Spread

Protein-Packed Smoothies:

- Banana Almond Protein Shake
- Blueberry Muffin Batter Smoothie
- Chocolate Peanut Butter Cup Shake

Indulgent Dessert Treats:

- Decadent Chocolate Avocado Mousse
- Mango Coconut Sorbet
- Raspberry Cheesecake Bliss

Hearty and Healthy Soups:

- Creamy Broccoli Cheddar Soup
- Butternut Squash and Apple Bisque
- Quinoa Vegetable Chowder

Unique Beverage Blends:

- Matcha Mint Mojito
- Turmeric Ginger Lemonade
- Pineapple Basil Sparkler

International Flavors:

- Thai Peanut Noodle Sauce
- Mexican Street Corn Dip
- Indian Spiced Mango Lassi

Quick and Easy Salsas:

- Fresh Mango Salsa
- Pineapple Cilantro Salsa
- Classic Tomato Salsa

Morning Energizers:

Sunrise Citrus Smoothie

Ingredients:

- 1 cup fresh orange juice
- 1/2 cup pineapple chunks (fresh or frozen)
- 1/2 cup mango chunks (fresh or frozen)
- 1 medium banana
- 1/2 cup Greek yogurt
- 1 tablespoon honey
- Ice cubes (optional)

Instructions:

Add the fresh orange juice to the blender.
Toss in the pineapple chunks and mango chunks.
Peel and add the banana to the mix.
Spoon in the Greek yogurt and drizzle the honey over the ingredients.
If you prefer a colder smoothie, add a handful of ice cubes.
Blend until smooth and creamy.
Pour into a glass, garnish with a slice of orange or a few fresh mint leaves, and enjoy the sunrise in a glass!

Note: Feel free to customize by adding a handful of spinach for an extra nutrient boost or a scoop of protein powder for added protein content.

Green Goddess Detox Blend

Ingredients:

- 1 cup coconut water
- 1 cup spinach leaves (fresh or frozen)
- 1/2 cucumber, peeled and sliced
- 1/2 green apple, cored and chopped
- 1/2 lemon, juiced
- 1 tablespoon chia seeds
- Fresh mint leaves for garnish
- Ice cubes (optional)

Instructions:

Pour coconut water into the blender.
Add spinach leaves, cucumber slices, and chopped green apple.
Squeeze in the juice from half a lemon.
Sprinkle chia seeds over the ingredients.
For a cooler blend, add a handful of ice cubes.
Blend until the mixture reaches a smooth consistency.
Pour into a glass, garnish with fresh mint leaves, and embrace the detoxifying goodness.

Note: Chia seeds add a delightful texture and are a great source of omega-3 fatty acids. Adjust the consistency by adding more coconut water if needed. This green goddess blend is an excellent way to kickstart your day or as a post-workout refresher.

Berry Burst Breakfast Bowl

Ingredients:

- 1 cup mixed berries (strawberries, blueberries, raspberries)
- 1 ripe banana, sliced
- 1/2 cup rolled oats
- 1/2 cup Greek yogurt
- 1 tablespoon honey
- 1 tablespoon chia seeds
- Granola for topping
- Fresh mint leaves for garnish

Instructions:

In a blender, combine mixed berries, sliced banana, rolled oats, Greek yogurt, honey, and chia seeds.
Blend until smooth and creamy.
Pour the mixture into a bowl.
Top with a generous sprinkle of granola for added crunch.
Garnish with additional berries and fresh mint leaves.
Dive into this burst of flavors, textures, and wholesome goodness.

Note: Customize your breakfast bowl with your favorite toppings like sliced almonds, coconut flakes, or a dollop of nut butter. This Berry Burst Breakfast Bowl is a delightful way to start your day with a nutritious and satisfying breakfast.

Smoothie Bowls Galore:

Tropical Paradise Bowl

Ingredients:

- 1 cup frozen mango chunks
- 1/2 cup frozen pineapple chunks
- 1/2 banana
- 1/2 cup coconut milk
- 1/4 cup Greek yogurt
- 1 tablespoon shredded coconut
- 1 tablespoon chia seeds
- Sliced kiwi and passion fruit for topping
- Granola for added crunch

Instructions:

In a blender, combine frozen mango chunks, frozen pineapple chunks, banana, coconut milk, and Greek yogurt.
Blend until smooth and creamy, adjusting the consistency with more coconut milk if needed.
Pour the smoothie into a bowl.
Top with shredded coconut, chia seeds, sliced kiwi, passion fruit, and a generous sprinkle of granola.
Serve immediately and transport yourself to a tropical paradise with every spoonful.

Note: Experiment with different tropical fruits like papaya, guava, or dragon fruit for a unique twist. Feel free to add a handful of spinach for an extra nutrient boost without compromising the tropical flavor. This Tropical Paradise Bowl is not only delicious but also a visual delight.

Acai Berry Bliss Bowl

Ingredients:

- 1 frozen acai berry packet
- 1/2 cup mixed berries (blueberries, strawberries, raspberries)
- 1/2 banana
- 1/2 cup almond milk
- 1 tablespoon almond butter
- 1 tablespoon honey
- Granola for topping
- Sliced strawberries and chia seeds for garnish

Instructions:

Run the frozen acai berry packet under warm water for a few seconds to slightly thaw it.
In a blender, combine the acai berry packet, mixed berries, banana, almond milk, almond butter, and honey.
Blend until smooth and creamy, adjusting the consistency with more almond milk if needed.
Pour the acai mixture into a bowl.
Top with granola, sliced strawberries, and a sprinkle of chia seeds for added texture.
Enjoy this Acai Berry Bliss Bowl as a nourishing and delightful breakfast or snack.

Note: Experiment with different toppings such as coconut flakes, sliced almonds, or a dollop of coconut yogurt. The versatility of this bowl makes it a favorite for acai enthusiasts, providing a perfect balance of sweetness and nutritional goodness.

Peanut Butter Power Bowl

Ingredients:

- 2 tablespoons creamy peanut butter
- 1 banana
- 1/2 cup Greek yogurt
- 1/4 cup rolled oats
- 1/2 cup almond milk
- 1 tablespoon honey
- Handful of crushed peanuts for topping
- Sliced banana and a drizzle of peanut butter for garnish

Instructions:

In a blender, combine creamy peanut butter, banana, Greek yogurt, rolled oats, almond milk, and honey.
Blend until the mixture is smooth and creamy.
Pour the peanut butter mixture into a bowl.
Top with a handful of crushed peanuts for added crunch.
Garnish with sliced banana and drizzle additional peanut butter on top.
Dive into this Peanut Butter Power Bowl for a delicious and satisfying breakfast or snack.

Note: Customize your bowl by adding a scoop of chocolate protein powder for a chocolate-peanut butter twist. You can also include sliced strawberries or a sprinkle of chia seeds for added variety. This power-packed bowl is a fantastic way to fuel your day with protein and energy.

Refreshing Cold Soups:

Chilled Cucumber Gazpacho

Ingredients:

- 2 large cucumbers, peeled and diced
- 4 ripe tomatoes, chopped
- 1/2 red bell pepper, diced
- 1/2 red onion, finely chopped
- 2 cloves garlic, minced
- 3 cups vegetable broth
- 1/4 cup red wine vinegar
- 1/4 cup extra-virgin olive oil
- 1 teaspoon salt, or to taste
- 1/2 teaspoon black pepper
- Fresh basil or mint leaves for garnish

Instructions:

> In a blender, combine cucumbers, tomatoes, red bell pepper, red onion, and garlic.
> Add vegetable broth, red wine vinegar, and extra-virgin olive oil to the blender.
> Season with salt and black pepper.
> Blend until the mixture reaches a smooth consistency.
> Taste and adjust the seasoning if needed.
> Chill the gazpacho in the refrigerator for at least 2 hours before serving.
> Garnish with fresh basil or mint leaves before serving.

Note: Customize your gazpacho by adding a dash of hot sauce for a spicy kick or a dollop of Greek yogurt for creaminess. Serve this Chilled Cucumber Gazpacho as a refreshing appetizer or light lunch on a warm day, and savor the cool, crisp flavors.

Spicy Watermelon Mint Soup

Ingredients:

- 4 cups seedless watermelon, diced
- 1 cucumber, peeled and diced
- 1 small red onion, finely chopped
- 1 jalapeño, seeds removed and minced
- 1/4 cup fresh mint leaves, chopped
- 2 tablespoons lime juice
- 1 tablespoon honey
- Salt to taste
- 1 cup cold water
- Ice cubes for serving
- Additional mint leaves for garnish

Instructions:

In a blender, combine diced watermelon, cucumber, red onion, minced jalapeño, and chopped mint leaves.
Add lime juice, honey, and a pinch of salt to the blender.
Pour in cold water to help with blending.
Blend until smooth and well combined.
Taste and adjust sweetness or spiciness if needed.
Chill the soup in the refrigerator for at least 1 hour.
Serve the Spicy Watermelon Mint Soup over ice cubes and garnish with additional mint leaves.

Note: For an extra layer of flavor, consider adding a splash of balsamic vinegar or a sprinkle of Tajin seasoning. This Spicy Watermelon Mint Soup is a perfect balance of sweet, savory, and spicy, making it an ideal summer treat or a unique appetizer for any occasion.

Creamy Avocado Lime Soup

Ingredients:

- 2 ripe avocados, peeled and pitted
- 1 cup plain Greek yogurt
- 2 cups vegetable broth
- 1/4 cup fresh cilantro, chopped
- 2 cloves garlic, minced
- Juice of 2 limes
- 1 tablespoon olive oil
- Salt and pepper to taste
- Sliced radishes and additional cilantro for garnish

Instructions:

In a blender, combine avocados, Greek yogurt, vegetable broth, cilantro, minced garlic, lime juice, and olive oil.
Blend until the mixture is smooth and creamy.
Season with salt and pepper to taste, adjusting as needed.
Chill the soup in the refrigerator for at least 2 hours.
Before serving, stir the soup well and adjust the consistency with a little extra broth if desired.
Ladle the Creamy Avocado Lime Soup into bowls and garnish with sliced radishes and additional cilantro.

Note: For an extra burst of flavor, consider adding a pinch of cayenne pepper for a subtle heat. This Creamy Avocado Lime Soup is a luxurious and nutritious option, perfect for a light lunch or an elegant appetizer at your next gathering.

Savory Dips and Spreads:

Roasted Red Pepper Hummus

Ingredients:

- 1 can (15 oz) chickpeas, drained and rinsed
- 1/2 cup roasted red peppers (from a jar or homemade)
- 1/4 cup tahini
- 2 cloves garlic, minced
- 3 tablespoons olive oil
- Juice of 1 lemon
- 1/2 teaspoon cumin
- Salt and pepper to taste
- Paprika and olive oil for garnish
- Chopped fresh parsley for garnish

Instructions:

In a food processor, combine chickpeas, roasted red peppers, tahini, minced garlic, olive oil, lemon juice, cumin, salt, and pepper.
Blend until the mixture is smooth and creamy, scraping down the sides as needed.
Taste and adjust the seasonings if necessary.
Transfer the hummus to a serving bowl.
Drizzle with olive oil, sprinkle with paprika, and garnish with chopped fresh parsley.
Serve the Roasted Red Pepper Hummus with pita chips, vegetable sticks, or as a spread for sandwiches.

Note: For an extra smoky flavor, you can add a pinch of smoked paprika or a splash of liquid smoke. This Roasted Red Pepper Hummus is a delightful way to enjoy a classic dip with a flavorful twist.

Spinach and Artichoke Dip

Ingredients:

- 1 cup frozen chopped spinach, thawed and drained
- 1 can (14 oz) artichoke hearts, drained and chopped
- 1 cup mayonnaise
- 1 cup sour cream
- 1 cup shredded mozzarella cheese
- 1 cup grated Parmesan cheese
- 1 teaspoon minced garlic
- 1/2 teaspoon onion powder
- Salt and pepper to taste
- Dash of hot sauce (optional)
- Tortilla chips or sliced baguette for serving

Instructions:

Preheat the oven to 375°F (190°C).
In a large mixing bowl, combine chopped spinach, chopped artichoke hearts, mayonnaise, sour cream, mozzarella cheese, Parmesan cheese, minced garlic, onion powder, salt, pepper, and hot sauce if using.
Mix until all ingredients are well combined.
Transfer the mixture to a baking dish, spreading it evenly.
Bake in the preheated oven for 25-30 minutes or until the dip is hot and bubbly, and the top is golden brown.
Remove from the oven and let it cool slightly before serving.
Serve the Spinach and Artichoke Dip with tortilla chips or sliced baguette.

Note: Customize by adding diced jalapeños for a spicy kick or a blend of different cheeses for extra richness. This Spinach and Artichoke Dip is a timeless favorite that's sure to please any crowd.

Zesty Black Bean Salsa

Ingredients:

- 1 can (15 oz) black beans, drained and rinsed
- 1 cup corn kernels (fresh, frozen, or canned)
- 1 cup cherry tomatoes, quartered
- 1/2 red onion, finely chopped
- 1 jalapeño, seeds removed and finely diced
- 1/4 cup fresh cilantro, chopped
- Juice of 2 limes
- 2 tablespoons extra-virgin olive oil
- 1 teaspoon ground cumin
- Salt and pepper to taste
- Avocado slices for garnish (optional)
- Tortilla chips for serving

Instructions:

In a large bowl, combine black beans, corn kernels, cherry tomatoes, red onion, jalapeño, and cilantro.
In a small bowl, whisk together lime juice, olive oil, ground cumin, salt, and pepper.
Pour the dressing over the black bean mixture and toss until well coated.
Adjust seasoning according to taste.
Cover the bowl and refrigerate for at least 30 minutes to let the flavors meld.
Before serving, garnish with avocado slices if desired.
Serve the Zesty Black Bean Salsa with tortilla chips or as a topping for grilled chicken or fish.

Note: Feel free to add diced mango or pineapple for a sweet twist or a dash of hot sauce for extra heat. This Zesty Black Bean Salsa is a crowd-pleaser that adds a refreshing kick to any occasion.

Creative Nut Butters:

Vanilla Almond Bliss Butter

Ingredients:

- 2 cups raw almonds
- 2 tablespoons coconut oil
- 2 tablespoons honey or maple syrup
- 1 teaspoon vanilla extract
- 1/4 teaspoon sea salt

Instructions:

> Preheat the oven to 350°F (175°C).
> Spread the raw almonds on a baking sheet in a single layer.
> Roast in the preheated oven for 10-12 minutes, stirring halfway through, until the almonds are fragrant and golden brown.
> Allow the almonds to cool for a few minutes.
> Transfer the roasted almonds to a food processor.
> Add coconut oil, honey or maple syrup, vanilla extract, and sea salt.
> Blend the mixture, stopping to scrape down the sides as needed, until it reaches a smooth and creamy consistency.
> Taste and adjust sweetness or saltiness as desired.
> Transfer the Vanilla Almond Bliss Butter to a jar and store in the refrigerator.

Note: Experiment with different types of honey or add a pinch of cinnamon for an extra layer of flavor. Spread this blissful butter on toast, swirl it into yogurt, or use it as a delicious dip for apple slices. The Vanilla Almond Bliss Butter is a delightful way to enjoy the wholesome goodness of nuts with a touch of sweetness.

Chocolate Hazelnut Heaven

Ingredients:

> 2 cups vanilla ice cream
> 1/2 cup milk
> 2 tablespoons chocolate syrup
> 3 tablespoons chocolate hazelnut spread (like Nutella)

1/4 cup crushed hazelnuts (optional, for garnish)
Whipped cream (optional, for topping)

Instructions:

In a blender, combine the vanilla ice cream, milk, chocolate syrup, and chocolate hazelnut spread.
Blend until smooth and creamy.
If you prefer a thicker consistency, you can add more ice cream. For a thinner shake, add more milk.
Pour the milkshake into glasses.
If desired, top with whipped cream and sprinkle crushed hazelnuts on top.
You can also drizzle a little extra chocolate syrup for an extra touch of indulgence.

Feel free to get creative and customize the recipe to suit your taste. You can add a banana for a banana-chocolate-hazelnut twist or even incorporate a shot of espresso for a caffeinated kick. Enjoy your Chocolate Hazelnut Heaven creation!

Maple Pecan Delight Spread

Ingredients:

1 cup pecans, toasted
1/4 cup maple syrup (adjust to taste)
2 tablespoons unsalted butter, softened
1/4 teaspoon vanilla extract
1/8 teaspoon salt (adjust to taste)

Instructions:

Toast the Pecans:
- Preheat your oven to 350°F (175°C).
- Spread the pecans on a baking sheet in a single layer.
- Toast in the preheated oven for about 8-10 minutes, or until fragrant. Make sure to stir them halfway through to ensure even toasting.
- Allow the toasted pecans to cool completely.

Prepare the Spread:
- In a food processor, add the cooled toasted pecans.
- Process until the pecans are finely chopped, resembling a coarse meal.

Add Flavors:
- Add the softened butter, maple syrup, vanilla extract, and salt to the chopped pecans in the food processor.

Blend:
- Process the mixture until it reaches a smooth, spreadable consistency. You may need to scrape down the sides of the food processor a few times to ensure everything is well combined.

Adjust to Taste:
- Taste the spread and adjust the sweetness or saltiness according to your preference. Add more maple syrup or salt if needed.

Store:
- Transfer the Maple Pecan Delight Spread to a jar or an airtight container.

This delightful spread can be stored in the refrigerator for a week or more. Spread it on toast, use it as a topping for pancakes or waffles, or enjoy it as a dip for apple slices or crackers. It's a perfect treat for a cozy breakfast or snack!

Protein-Packed Smoothies:

Banana Almond Protein Shake

Ingredients:

- 1 ripe banana
- 1 cup almond milk (or any milk of your choice)
- 1 scoop vanilla protein powder
- 1 tablespoon almond butter
- 1/2 teaspoon cinnamon (optional)
- Ice cubes (optional)

Instructions:

Prepare Ingredients:
- Peel the ripe banana and break it into a few chunks.

Blend:
- In a blender, combine the banana chunks, almond milk, vanilla protein powder, almond butter, and cinnamon (if using).
- If you prefer a colder and thicker shake, add a handful of ice cubes.

Blend Until Smooth:
- Blend the ingredients until smooth and creamy. Make sure all the ingredients are well incorporated.

Adjust Consistency:
- If the shake is too thick, you can add more almond milk in small increments until you reach your desired consistency.

Taste and Adjust:
- Taste the shake and adjust the sweetness or thickness by adding more banana, protein powder, or almond butter as needed.

Serve:
- Pour the Banana Almond Protein Shake into a glass.

Optional Garnish:
- Optionally, you can sprinkle a little cinnamon on top or add a few slices of banana for garnish.

This protein-packed smoothie is not only delicious but also a great way to refuel your body after a workout or to kickstart your day with a nutritious breakfast. Adjust the ingredients to suit your taste preferences and nutritional needs. Enjoy your Banana Almond Protein Shake!

Blueberry Muffin Batter Smoothie

Ingredients:

    1 cup frozen blueberries
    1 ripe banana
    1/2 cup rolled oats
    1 cup vanilla yogurt (Greek yogurt for added protein)
    1/2 cup milk (dairy or plant-based)
    1 tablespoon honey or maple syrup (optional, for added sweetness)
    1/2 teaspoon vanilla extract
    A pinch of cinnamon (optional)
    Ice cubes (optional)

Instructions:

    Prepare Ingredients:
- Peel the banana and break it into a few chunks.

    Blend:
- In a blender, combine the frozen blueberries, banana chunks, rolled oats, vanilla yogurt, milk, honey or maple syrup (if using), vanilla extract, and cinnamon (if using).
- If you prefer a colder and thicker smoothie, add some ice cubes.

    Blend Until Smooth:
- Blend the ingredients until you achieve a smooth and creamy consistency. Ensure that the oats are well blended.

    Taste and Adjust:
- Taste the smoothie and adjust the sweetness or thickness by adding more honey, maple syrup, or oats as needed.

    Serve:
- Pour the Blueberry Muffin Batter Smoothie into a glass.

    Optional Garnish:
- Optionally, you can sprinkle a few additional blueberries on top or add a light dusting of cinnamon for a decorative touch.

This smoothie captures the essence of a blueberry muffin and is a great way to incorporate wholesome ingredients into your breakfast or snack. Feel free to customize the recipe to suit your taste preferences. Enjoy your Blueberry Muffin Batter Smoothie!

Chocolate Peanut Butter Cup Shake

Ingredients:

2 cups chocolate ice cream
1 cup milk (dairy or plant-based)
2 tablespoons creamy peanut butter
2 tablespoons chocolate syrup
1/2 teaspoon vanilla extract
Whipped cream (for topping, optional)
Chopped peanuts or chocolate shavings (for garnish, optional)

Instructions:

Prepare Ingredients:
- Allow the chocolate ice cream to soften slightly for easier blending.
- Measure out the milk, peanut butter, chocolate syrup, and vanilla extract.

Blend:
- In a blender, combine the chocolate ice cream, milk, peanut butter, chocolate syrup, and vanilla extract.
- Blend until the mixture is smooth and creamy.

Adjust Consistency:
- If the shake is too thick, you can add more milk, a little at a time, until you reach your desired consistency.

Taste and Adjust:
- Taste the shake and adjust the sweetness or peanut butter flavor by adding more chocolate syrup or peanut butter if desired.

Serve:
- Pour the Chocolate Peanut Butter Cup Shake into a glass.

Optional Toppings:
- Top the shake with whipped cream for an extra indulgence.
- Garnish with chopped peanuts or chocolate shavings for added texture and visual appeal.

Enjoy:
- Grab a straw and enjoy your delicious Chocolate Peanut Butter Cup Shake!

Feel free to get creative and customize this shake to suit your preferences. You can also add a frozen banana for a thicker consistency or incorporate a handful of ice cubes for extra chill. It's a perfect treat for chocolate and peanut butter enthusiasts!

Indulgent Dessert Treats:

Decadent Chocolate Avocado Mousse

Ingredients:

   2 ripe avocados
   1/2 cup unsweetened cocoa powder
   1/2 cup maple syrup or agave nectar
   1/4 cup almond milk (or any milk of your choice)
   1 teaspoon vanilla extract
   A pinch of salt
   Optional toppings: whipped cream, berries, or shaved chocolate

Instructions:

   Prepare Avocados:
   - Cut the avocados in half, remove the pits, and scoop the flesh into a blender or food processor.

   Blend Avocado Mixture:
   - Add cocoa powder, maple syrup (or agave nectar), almond milk, vanilla extract, and a pinch of salt to the blender or food processor with the avocados.

   Blend Until Smooth:
   - Blend the ingredients until the mixture becomes smooth and creamy. You may need to stop and scrape down the sides a few times to ensure everything is well combined.

   Taste and Adjust:
   - Taste the chocolate avocado mousse and adjust the sweetness or chocolate intensity according to your preference. Add more maple syrup or cocoa powder if needed.

   Chill:
   - Transfer the mousse to serving bowls or glasses and refrigerate for at least 1-2 hours to allow it to chill and firm up.

   Serve:
   - Once chilled, you can serve the Decadent Chocolate Avocado Mousse on its own or with your favorite toppings.

   Optional Toppings:

- Before serving, you can add a dollop of whipped cream on top or garnish with fresh berries or shaved chocolate.

This Chocolate Avocado Mousse is a delightful way to enjoy a rich and creamy dessert with the added nutritional benefits of avocados. It's perfect for satisfying your chocolate cravings in a healthier way. Enjoy this decadent treat!

Mango Coconut Sorbet

Ingredients:

3 cups ripe mango, peeled and diced (about 3 medium-sized mangoes)
1 cup coconut milk (full-fat for creamier texture)
1/2 cup granulated sugar (adjust to taste)
1 tablespoon lime juice (optional, for a hint of citrus)
Shredded coconut or mint leaves for garnish (optional)

Instructions:

Prepare Mango:
- Peel and dice the ripe mangoes.

Blend Ingredients:
- In a blender, combine the diced mango, coconut milk, sugar, and lime juice (if using).
- Blend until the mixture is smooth and well combined.

Taste and Adjust:
- Taste the mixture and adjust the sweetness by adding more sugar if needed. Blend again to combine.

Chill:
- Pour the sorbet mixture into a bowl and refrigerate for at least 2 hours to chill.

Churn (Optional):
- If you have an ice cream maker, you can churn the chilled mixture according to the manufacturer's instructions for a creamier texture. If not, proceed to the next step.

Freeze:
- Transfer the chilled or churned mixture into a shallow, airtight container. Ensure it's spread evenly.

Freeze Again:
- Freeze the mixture for at least 4-6 hours or overnight until it reaches a sorbet-like consistency.

Serve:
- Before serving, let the sorbet sit at room temperature for a few minutes to soften slightly.
- Scoop the Mango Coconut Sorbet into bowls or cones.

Garnish (Optional):
- Garnish with shredded coconut or mint leaves for a decorative touch.

Enjoy the tropical goodness of Mango Coconut Sorbet on a hot day or as a light and refreshing dessert after a meal!

Raspberry Cheesecake Bliss

Ingredients:

For the Cheesecake Base:

    2 cups cream cheese, softened
    1/2 cup granulated sugar
    1 teaspoon vanilla extract
    1/4 cup sour cream
    Zest of one lemon (optional)
    Graham cracker crust or crushed graham crackers for the base

For the Raspberry Swirl:

    1 cup fresh or frozen raspberries
    2 tablespoons granulated sugar
    1 tablespoon water
    1 tablespoon lemon juice

Instructions:

Cheesecake Base:

    Prepare Graham Cracker Base:
- If you're using a graham cracker crust, press it into the base of your serving dish. If using crushed graham crackers, mix them with melted butter and press the mixture into the base.

    Prepare Cheesecake Filling:
- In a bowl, beat the cream cheese until smooth and creamy.
- Add sugar, vanilla extract, sour cream, and lemon zest (if using). Beat until well combined and smooth.

    Layer the Cheesecake Base:
- Spread the cream cheese mixture over the graham cracker base, smoothing the top with a spatula.

Raspberry Swirl:

    Prepare Raspberry Sauce:

- In a saucepan, combine raspberries, sugar, water, and lemon juice. Cook over medium heat until the raspberries break down and the mixture thickens slightly (about 5-7 minutes).

Strain the Raspberry Sauce:
- Strain the raspberry sauce through a fine mesh sieve to remove seeds, collecting the smooth raspberry puree.

Swirl in the Raspberry Sauce:
- Spoon dollops of the raspberry puree onto the cheesecake base. Use a knife or skewer to create swirls by gently dragging it through the raspberry puree.

Chill:
- Refrigerate the Raspberry Cheesecake Bliss for at least 4-6 hours or overnight to allow it to set.

Serve:
- Once set, cut into squares or slices and serve chilled.

Optional Garnish:
- Garnish with fresh raspberries, a drizzle of raspberry sauce, or a dusting of powdered sugar before serving.

Enjoy the blissful combination of creamy cheesecake and the fruity goodness of raspberries with this Raspberry Cheesecake Bliss!

Hearty and Healthy Soups:

Creamy Broccoli Cheddar Soup

Ingredients:

    2 tablespoons olive oil
    1 onion, finely chopped
    2 cloves garlic, minced
    3 cups fresh broccoli florets, chopped
    2 medium carrots, peeled and diced
    3 tablespoons all-purpose flour
    4 cups low-sodium vegetable or chicken broth
    2 cups milk (whole or 2%)
    2 cups shredded sharp cheddar cheese
    Salt and black pepper to taste
    1/2 teaspoon nutmeg (optional, for added warmth)
    Croutons or additional shredded cheese for garnish (optional)

Instructions:

Sauté Vegetables:
- In a large pot, heat the olive oil over medium heat. Add chopped onions and cook until softened, about 3-5 minutes.
- Add minced garlic and cook for an additional 1-2 minutes until fragrant.

Add Broccoli and Carrots:
- Add chopped broccoli and diced carrots to the pot. Stir and cook for another 5 minutes until the vegetables begin to soften.

Make Roux:
- Sprinkle the flour over the vegetables and stir to coat. Cook for 2-3 minutes to remove the raw taste of the flour.

Add Broth and Milk:
- Gradually pour in the vegetable or chicken broth, stirring constantly to avoid lumps from forming.
- Add milk to the pot and continue stirring. Bring the mixture to a gentle boil, then reduce the heat to simmer.

Simmer:
- Let the soup simmer for about 15-20 minutes, or until the vegetables are tender.

Blend (Optional):
- For a smoother texture, use an immersion blender to blend the soup until it reaches your desired consistency. Alternatively, transfer a portion of the soup to a blender and blend, then return it to the pot.

Add Cheddar Cheese:
- Stir in the shredded cheddar cheese until melted and well combined.

Season:
- Season the soup with salt, black pepper, and nutmeg (if using). Adjust the seasoning to your taste.

Serve:
- Ladle the Creamy Broccoli Cheddar Soup into bowls. Garnish with croutons or additional shredded cheese if desired.

This hearty and healthy soup is a comforting option for a satisfying meal. Enjoy the warm and creamy goodness of this Creamy Broccoli Cheddar Soup!

Butternut Squash and Apple Bisque

Ingredients:

1 medium-sized butternut squash, peeled, seeded, and diced
2 medium-sized apples, peeled, cored, and chopped
1 large onion, chopped
2 cloves garlic, minced
2 carrots, peeled and chopped
4 cups vegetable or chicken broth
1 cup apple juice or apple cider
1 teaspoon ground cinnamon
1/2 teaspoon ground nutmeg
Salt and pepper to taste
2 tablespoons olive oil
1 cup coconut milk or heavy cream (optional, for added creaminess)
Chopped fresh parsley or chives for garnish

Instructions:

Prepare Vegetables:
- In a large pot, heat olive oil over medium heat. Add chopped onions, garlic, and carrots. Cook until the onions are translucent, about 5 minutes.

Add Squash and Apples:
- Add the diced butternut squash and chopped apples to the pot. Cook for an additional 5-7 minutes, stirring occasionally.

Season:
- Sprinkle ground cinnamon, nutmeg, salt, and pepper over the vegetables. Stir to coat evenly.

Add Broth and Apple Juice:
- Pour in the vegetable or chicken broth and apple juice. Bring the mixture to a boil.

Simmer:
- Reduce the heat to low, cover the pot, and let the soup simmer for about 20-25 minutes, or until the squash and apples are tender.

Blend:

- Use an immersion blender to puree the soup until smooth. Alternatively, transfer the soup in batches to a blender, blend until smooth, and return it to the pot.

Add Cream (Optional):
- Stir in coconut milk or heavy cream if you want a creamier bisque. Adjust the consistency with more broth if needed.

Adjust Seasoning:
- Taste the bisque and adjust the seasoning as necessary.

Serve:
- Ladle the Butternut Squash and Apple Bisque into bowls. Garnish with chopped fresh parsley or chives.

This bisque is perfect for a cozy fall or winter meal. The combination of butternut squash and apples creates a harmonious blend of flavors that's both satisfying and nutritious. Enjoy your delicious and comforting bisque!

Quinoa Vegetable Chowder

Ingredients:

1 cup quinoa, rinsed
1 tablespoon olive oil
1 onion, diced
2 carrots, peeled and chopped
2 celery stalks, chopped
2 cloves garlic, minced
1 teaspoon dried thyme
1 teaspoon ground cumin
4 cups vegetable broth
1 can (14 oz) diced tomatoes, undrained
1 cup corn kernels (fresh, frozen, or canned)
1 cup diced potatoes
1 cup broccoli florets
Salt and pepper to taste
2 cups milk (dairy or plant-based)
1/2 cup grated cheddar cheese (optional, for garnish)
Chopped fresh parsley or green onions for garnish

Instructions:

Rinse Quinoa:
- Rinse quinoa under cold water and set aside.

Sauté Vegetables:
- In a large pot, heat olive oil over medium heat. Add diced onion, carrots, and celery. Sauté until the vegetables are softened, about 5-7 minutes.

Add Aromatics:
- Add minced garlic, dried thyme, and ground cumin. Stir and cook for an additional 1-2 minutes until fragrant.

Add Quinoa and Broth:
- Add rinsed quinoa to the pot. Pour in the vegetable broth and bring the mixture to a boil.

Add Tomatoes and Vegetables:
- Add diced tomatoes (with their juice), corn kernels, diced potatoes, and broccoli florets. Stir to combine.

Simmer:

- Reduce the heat to low, cover the pot, and let the soup simmer for about 15-20 minutes or until the quinoa and vegetables are cooked through.

Season:
- Season the chowder with salt and pepper according to your taste.

Add Milk:
- Pour in the milk and stir well. Let the chowder simmer for an additional 5 minutes to heat through.

Garnish and Serve:
- Ladle the Quinoa Vegetable Chowder into bowls. Garnish with grated cheddar cheese, chopped fresh parsley, or green onions if desired.

This Quinoa Vegetable Chowder is a wholesome and filling meal that's packed with fiber, protein, and vitamins. It's perfect for a comforting and nutritious lunch or dinner. Enjoy!

Unique Beverage Blends:

Matcha Mint Mojito

Ingredients:

- 1 teaspoon matcha powder
- 2 teaspoons honey or agave syrup (adjust to taste)
- 8-10 fresh mint leaves
- 1 tablespoon lime juice
- 1 cup ice cubes
- 1/4 cup white rum (optional, for an alcoholic version)
- Club soda or sparkling water
- Lime wedges and mint sprigs for garnish

Instructions:

Prepare Matcha Paste:
- In a small bowl, mix the matcha powder with a small amount of water to create a smooth paste.

Muddle Mint:
- In a glass, muddle the fresh mint leaves to release their flavor. Use a muddler or the back of a spoon.

Add Matcha Paste:
- Add the matcha paste to the glass with the muddled mint.

Sweeten:
- Pour honey or agave syrup into the glass. Adjust the sweetness to your liking.

Add Lime Juice:
- Squeeze fresh lime juice into the glass.

Mix:
- Stir the ingredients together to combine the matcha, mint, honey, and lime juice.

Add Ice:
- Fill the glass with ice cubes.

Optional: Add Rum for Alcoholic Version:
- If you want an alcoholic version, pour in the white rum and stir.

Top with Club Soda:

- Pour club soda or sparkling water into the glass, filling it to the top.

Stir Gently:
- Gently stir the ingredients to combine and chill the drink.

Garnish:
- Garnish the Matcha Mint Mojito with lime wedges and a sprig of fresh mint.

Serve:
- Serve the Matcha Mint Mojito immediately and enjoy the unique blend of flavors.

This Matcha Mint Mojito is a vibrant and energizing beverage that's perfect for a sunny day or as a refreshing pick-me-up. Adjust the sweetness and matcha intensity according to your taste preferences. Cheers!

Turmeric Ginger Lemonade

Ingredients:

- 4 cups cold water
- 1 tablespoon fresh turmeric, grated (or 1 teaspoon ground turmeric)
- 1 tablespoon fresh ginger, grated
- 1/2 cup fresh lemon juice (about 3-4 lemons)
- 1/4 cup honey or maple syrup (adjust to taste)
- Ice cubes
- Lemon slices and mint leaves for garnish (optional)

Instructions:

Prepare Turmeric and Ginger:
- Peel and grate fresh turmeric and ginger. If using ground turmeric, skip this step.

Make Turmeric Ginger Base:
- In a pitcher, combine cold water, grated turmeric, and grated ginger. Stir well.

Add Lemon Juice:
- Squeeze fresh lemon juice into the pitcher.

Sweeten:
- Add honey or maple syrup to the pitcher, adjusting the sweetness to your liking. Stir until the sweetener dissolves.

Mix Well:
- Mix the ingredients well to ensure the turmeric, ginger, and sweetener are evenly distributed.

Chill:
- Refrigerate the turmeric ginger lemonade for at least 1-2 hours to allow the flavors to meld.

Strain (Optional):
- If you prefer a smoother lemonade, strain the mixture using a fine mesh sieve or cheesecloth to remove the turmeric and ginger bits.

Serve Over Ice:
- Fill glasses with ice cubes and pour the turmeric ginger lemonade over the ice.

Garnish (Optional):

- Garnish with lemon slices and mint leaves for a fresh and decorative touch.

Stir Before Serving:
- Stir the lemonade before serving to distribute any settled ingredients.

Enjoy:
- Refresh yourself with a glass of Turmeric Ginger Lemonade. Sip and savor the bright and invigorating flavors.

This Turmeric Ginger Lemonade not only quenches your thirst but also provides potential health benefits from the turmeric and ginger. It's a perfect drink for warm days or whenever you want a revitalizing beverage.

Pineapple Basil Sparkler

Ingredients:

- 2 cups fresh pineapple chunks
- 1/4 cup fresh basil leaves, plus extra for garnish
- 2 tablespoons honey or agave syrup (adjust to taste)
- 1 tablespoon fresh lime juice
- 2 cups sparkling water or club soda
- Ice cubes
- Pineapple slices for garnish (optional)

Instructions:

Prepare Pineapple and Basil:
- Peel and chop fresh pineapple into chunks.
- Wash and pat dry the basil leaves.

Make Pineapple Basil Base:
- In a blender, combine fresh pineapple chunks, basil leaves, honey or agave syrup, and fresh lime juice.
- Blend until smooth to create the pineapple basil puree.

Strain (Optional):
- If you prefer a smoother drink, you can strain the puree using a fine mesh sieve or cheesecloth to remove any pulp.

Assemble the Sparkler:
- Fill glasses with ice cubes.
- Pour 1/4 to 1/2 cup of the pineapple basil puree into each glass, depending on your taste preference.

Add Sparkling Water:
- Top each glass with sparkling water or club soda.

Stir Gently:
- Gently stir the mixture in each glass to combine the puree with the sparkling water.

Garnish:
- Garnish the Pineapple Basil Sparkler with additional basil leaves and pineapple slices if desired.

Serve:
- Serve the sparkler immediately and enjoy the tropical and herbaceous flavors.

This Pineapple Basil Sparkler is a perfect non-alcoholic beverage for a warm day or as a refreshing mocktail for any occasion. It's a fantastic combination of sweet, citrusy pineapple and aromatic basil, creating a drink that's both tasty and visually appealing. Cheers!

International Flavors:

Thai Peanut Noodle Sauce

Ingredients:

> 1/2 cup creamy peanut butter
> 3 tablespoons soy sauce (use tamari for a gluten-free option)
> 2 tablespoons rice vinegar
> 2 tablespoons sesame oil
> 2 tablespoons honey or maple syrup
> 1 tablespoon fresh lime juice
> 2 teaspoons minced garlic
> 1 teaspoon grated ginger
> 1/2 teaspoon red pepper flakes (adjust to taste)
> 1/4 cup warm water (to thin the sauce, as needed)

Instructions:

> Combine Ingredients:
> - In a bowl, whisk together peanut butter, soy sauce, rice vinegar, sesame oil, honey or maple syrup, lime juice, minced garlic, grated ginger, and red pepper flakes.
>
> Adjust Consistency:
> - If the sauce is too thick, add warm water, one tablespoon at a time, until you reach your desired consistency. Whisk well to combine.
>
> Taste and Adjust:
> - Taste the sauce and adjust the flavor to your liking. You can add more soy sauce for saltiness, honey for sweetness, lime juice for acidity, or red pepper flakes for heat.
>
> Use or Store:
> - The Thai Peanut Noodle Sauce is now ready to use. You can toss it with cooked noodles, use it as a dip for spring rolls, drizzle it over a salad, or incorporate it into stir-fries.
>
> Store:
> - Store any leftover sauce in an airtight container in the refrigerator for up to a week.

Optional Additions:

- If you want to enhance the flavors, consider adding a tablespoon of fish sauce for umami or a dash of sriracha for extra heat.

This Thai Peanut Noodle Sauce brings a perfect balance of savory, sweet, and spicy notes to your dishes. Feel free to adjust the ingredients to suit your taste preferences, and enjoy the rich and authentic flavors of Thai cuisine!

Mexican Street Corn Dip

Ingredients:

4 cups corn kernels (fresh or frozen)
1/2 cup mayonnaise
1/2 cup sour cream
1 cup crumbled cotija cheese (reserve some for garnish)
1/2 cup finely chopped fresh cilantro
1/2 teaspoon chili powder
1/4 teaspoon cayenne pepper (optional, for extra heat)
1 clove garlic, minced
1 tablespoon lime juice
Salt and pepper to taste
Tortilla chips or sliced baguette for serving

Instructions:

Grill or Saute Corn:
- If using fresh corn, grill or sauté the corn kernels until they develop a slightly charred appearance. If using frozen corn, cook according to package instructions.

Prepare the Dip:
- In a large bowl, combine the grilled or sautéed corn with mayonnaise, sour cream, crumbled cotija cheese, chopped cilantro, chili powder, cayenne pepper (if using), minced garlic, lime juice, salt, and pepper.

Mix Well:
- Stir the ingredients until well combined. Ensure that the mayonnaise, sour cream, and cheese coat the corn evenly.

Adjust Seasoning:
- Taste the dip and adjust the seasoning as needed. You can add more lime juice, salt, or spices to suit your taste.

Chill:
- Refrigerate the Mexican Street Corn Dip for at least 30 minutes to allow the flavors to meld.

Garnish:
- Before serving, garnish the dip with an extra sprinkle of crumbled cotija cheese and additional chopped cilantro.

Serve:
- Serve the Mexican Street Corn Dip with tortilla chips or sliced baguette.

This creamy and flavorful dip captures the essence of elote, the beloved Mexican street food. It's perfect for parties, gatherings, or as a delicious snack. Enjoy the delicious taste of Mexican street corn in dip form!

Indian Spiced Mango Lassi

Ingredients:

2 cups ripe mango, peeled and diced (fresh or frozen)
1 cup plain yogurt (Greek yogurt for a thicker consistency)
1/2 cup milk (dairy or plant-based)
2 tablespoons honey or sugar (adjust to taste)
1/2 teaspoon ground cardamom
1/4 teaspoon ground cinnamon
A pinch of ground ginger (optional)
Ice cubes (optional)
Chopped pistachios or mint leaves for garnish (optional)

Instructions:

Prepare Mango:
- Peel and dice the ripe mango. If using frozen mango, ensure it's thawed.

Blend Ingredients:
- In a blender, combine the diced mango, plain yogurt, milk, honey or sugar, ground cardamom, ground cinnamon, and ground ginger (if using).

Blend Until Smooth:
- Blend the ingredients until you achieve a smooth and creamy consistency.

Adjust Sweetness:
- Taste the lassi and adjust the sweetness by adding more honey or sugar if needed. Blend again to combine.

Add Ice (Optional):
- If you prefer a colder and thicker lassi, add ice cubes to the blender and blend until the ice is crushed.

Serve:
- Pour the Indian Spiced Mango Lassi into glasses.

Garnish (Optional):
- Garnish with chopped pistachios or mint leaves for added texture and freshness.

Enjoy:
- Serve the Mango Lassi immediately and enjoy the delightful blend of mango and spices.

This Indian Spiced Mango Lassi is a perfect beverage to cool down on a warm day or complement a spicy Indian meal. The combination of sweet mango with the warmth of cardamom and cinnamon creates a harmonious and flavorful drink. Cheers!

Quick and Easy Salsas:

Fresh Mango Salsa

Ingredients:

> 2 ripe mangoes, peeled, pitted, and diced
> 1/2 red onion, finely chopped
> 1 jalapeño pepper, seeds removed and finely chopped
> 1 red bell pepper, diced
> 1/4 cup fresh cilantro, chopped
> Juice of 1 lime
> Salt and pepper to taste

Instructions:

> Prepare Ingredients:
> - Peel, pit, and dice the ripe mangoes.
> - Finely chop the red onion.
> - Remove the seeds from the jalapeño and finely chop it.
> - Dice the red bell pepper.
> - Chop the fresh cilantro.
>
> Combine Ingredients:
> - In a bowl, combine the diced mangoes, chopped red onion, jalapeño, red bell pepper, and cilantro.
>
> Add Lime Juice:
> - Squeeze the juice of one lime over the mango mixture.
>
> Season:
> - Season the salsa with salt and pepper to taste. Adjust the seasoning according to your preference.
>
> Mix Well:
> - Gently toss all the ingredients together until well combined.
>
> Chill (Optional):
> - If time allows, refrigerate the mango salsa for about 15-30 minutes to let the flavors meld.
>
> Serve:
> - Serve the Fresh Mango Salsa as a topping for grilled chicken or fish, as a dip with tortilla chips, or as a side dish to complement various meals.

Enjoy:
- Enjoy the vibrant and tropical flavors of Fresh Mango Salsa!

This Fresh Mango Salsa is not only quick and easy to prepare but also versatile. Its sweet and tangy profile makes it a delightful addition to many dishes, from tacos and grilled meats to salads and seafood. Feel free to customize the recipe by adding ingredients like diced avocado, black beans, or lime zest for extra flair!

Pineapple Cilantro Salsa

Ingredients:

1 cup fresh pineapple, diced
1/2 red onion, finely chopped
1 jalapeño pepper, seeds removed and finely chopped
1/4 cup fresh cilantro, chopped
Juice of 1 lime
Salt and pepper to taste

Instructions:

Prepare Ingredients:
- Dice the fresh pineapple into small, bite-sized pieces.
- Finely chop the red onion.
- Remove the seeds from the jalapeño and finely chop it.
- Chop the fresh cilantro.

Combine Ingredients:
- In a bowl, combine the diced pineapple, chopped red onion, chopped jalapeño, and cilantro.

Add Lime Juice:
- Squeeze the juice of one lime over the pineapple mixture.

Season:
- Season the salsa with salt and pepper to taste. Adjust the seasoning according to your preference.

Mix Well:
- Gently toss all the ingredients together until well combined.

Chill (Optional):
- If time allows, refrigerate the Pineapple Cilantro Salsa for about 15-30 minutes to let the flavors meld.

Serve:
- Serve the Pineapple Cilantro Salsa as a topping for grilled chicken or fish, as a dip with tortilla chips, or as a side dish to complement various meals.

Enjoy:
- Enjoy the tropical and vibrant flavors of Pineapple Cilantro Salsa!

This salsa brings together the sweetness of pineapple with the freshness of cilantro and a hint of heat from the jalapeño. It's a versatile and delicious condiment that adds a burst of flavor to your favorite dishes. Feel free to customize the recipe by adding ingredients like diced red bell pepper, lime zest, or a touch of honey for added sweetness!

Classic Tomato Salsa

Ingredients:

- 4 medium-sized tomatoes, diced
- 1/2 red onion, finely chopped
- 1 jalapeño pepper, seeds removed and finely chopped
- 2 cloves garlic, minced
- 1/4 cup fresh cilantro, chopped
- Juice of 1 lime
- Salt and pepper to taste

Instructions:

Prepare Ingredients:
- Dice the tomatoes into small pieces.
- Finely chop the red onion and jalapeño.
- Mince the garlic.
- Chop the fresh cilantro.

Combine Ingredients:
- In a bowl, combine the diced tomatoes, chopped red onion, chopped jalapeño, minced garlic, and chopped cilantro.

Add Lime Juice:
- Squeeze the juice of one lime over the tomato mixture.

Season:
- Season the salsa with salt and pepper to taste. Adjust the seasoning according to your preference.

Mix Well:
- Gently toss all the ingredients together until well combined.

Chill (Optional):
- If time allows, refrigerate the Classic Tomato Salsa for about 15-30 minutes to let the flavors meld.

Serve:
- Serve the salsa with tortilla chips, as a topping for tacos, or as a side dish for your favorite Mexican meals.

Enjoy:
- Enjoy the fresh and zesty flavors of Classic Tomato Salsa!

Feel free to customize the recipe to your liking by adding ingredients like diced green bell pepper, a dash of cumin, or a pinch of red pepper flakes for extra heat. This classic tomato salsa is a versatile and timeless favorite that's sure to be a hit at any gathering!

www.ingramcontent.com/pod-product-compliance
Lightning Source LLC
LaVergne TN
LVHW081332060526
838201LV00055B/2586